DEFINING CHIC

CARRIER AND COMPANY INTERIORS

PAUL ETIENNE SAIN
COLLABORATEURS
HENRI TAMBUTE
AVEC
JACQUES BADEREL
ROBERT BAUMEAU
CLÉMENT DURLIN
MCMLII

DEFINING CHIC
CARRIER AND COMPANY INTERIORS

Jesse Carrier and Mara Miller

written with Judith Nasatir

RIZZOLI
NEW YORK

New York · Paris · London · Milan

CONTENTS

INTRODUCTION

Being a designer is a bit like being a Method actor inhabiting a role. At least, that's been our experience since we launched our firm nearly twenty years ago. Our goal from the start has been to create chic, timeless, uniquely personal homes for each client. This means that we find ourselves slipping in and out of different lives and lifestyles with every project. The only way we know to ensure that we make the best, most beautiful choices for that client from the oceans of possibilities is to understand their personal preferences, dreams, aspirations, needs, and lifestyles. So we dig deep. Then we filter what we've unearthed through the practical knowledge of design to express that client's individual vision in an appropriate aesthetic language and make their home function seamlessly to enhance their family's daily experience. Like the Method actor, we live vicariously through them for the duration of the project—but for their fulfillment, not for our own. This detachment, the lack of an agenda other than providing superlative service, allows us to pivot with each new client and vision, as the broad range and scope of projects in this book make clear.

Every client comes to us with a point of view, with some idea of what they hope to achieve, of how they want to live in and use their home, even if it's just a few words or images. We learned very early on in our careers that everyone interprets luxury in their own way. The history of design and the chronicles of evolving styles tell us the same story: there is no one right way, no sole absolute aesthetic, no single best look. Creativity for us means keeping an open mind. We approach each project without preconceptions, stylistic or otherwise. What matters is what is appropriate for the person, place, and time.

Successful projects inevitably balance the creative vision with the functional necessities. Our goal is to build the dream within strict practical parameters. Our approach is to make the home as personal as possible, not just designed. Some people want their interiors to be visually over the top.

Others have a taste for the understated. There is always a balance between what feels comfortable to the client, and what they want us to make them comfortable with, which is really the reason why they came to us in the first place. Whatever the client's taste and lifestyle—in broad terms, formal or informal, traditional or contemporary—we pour time, deep thought, and great care into making the countless decisions and endless choices that ultimately come together to create their living environment.

We do feel strongly, though, that there's a certain visual language that is tethered to the project's context: to its specific location and type of architecture. We bring that vocabulary and grammar of appropriateness and our imaginations to bear, and we consider all the potential variables. A classic country colonial in Connecticut calls for one paradigm, whereas a cedar-shingled cottage in the Hamptons suggests another. A town house on New York's Upper East Side insists on a level of chic no matter the style, while a contemporary hacienda with an art deco-era core in Southern California also wants a high level of sophistication and casual comfort. An apartment in a turn-of-the-century New York building replete with many vestiges of its original period architecture seems to require a certain measure of romance, while, just up the avenue, a modernized duplex in a prewar Manhattan aerie on Central Park calls for a different degree of historical resonance.

Translating concepts and ideas into the reality of fabrics, forms, furnishings, and finishes is a fluid process. But it is also a formula. So many options exist that we might like, or that might be aesthetically pleasing, or appropriate, but that in our view are just too typical, expected, or trendy. It matters to us that each selection is particular and personal, that every choice is the right choice for the unique place and special environment we are working to create for that specific client. We want the homes we design for our clients to be more than aesthetically pleasing. In our view, ease of use is intrinsic to the idea of custom design. And custom in our vocabulary means personalized, not just individualized. We care deeply that the spaces we create are comfortable, that they function effortlessly for the lives they support, and that they are never under-decorated or overdesigned.

Every project is an interesting adventure. And they often have very similar sets of issues that arise out of the unknowns. As different as each project may be from all the others, the process is always comparable. Along the way, we happily find ourselves explaining, answering questions, and introducing an expanded range of possibilities. Partly, this is because we truly are design geeks, and we love to drill down and share the minutiae. But we also know that an important part of our role is to open our clients' eyes to options that they may not realize exist.

Creating a home is always more than an additive and subtractive process. In making sure that the whole becomes more than the sum of its individual pieces, we look for the touches—some incredibly discrete and tiny; others much more foundational—that can have an outsize impact, that will lift the overall effect. Early in our careers we realized that details can speak, they can scream, or they can whisper. But it's not just the details. Every aspect, every facet of a space affects all the others because design is a matter of relationships. We keep looking until we find the level of quality that we insist on, and then we take it a little farther. We can do this because we trust in each other's confidence in the process, in the broadness of each other's outlook and approach, and in the clarity and specificity of the decision-making that result from our partnership.

We're practical people. We're practical designers. We're all for a practical solution—the practical solution that's beautiful. Every designer in the world wants their clients to experience that amazing moment of truth when they walk through their new home for the first time, and every day after: that they've entered a world made just for them that's beyond their wildest dreams, and beyond anything they could have imagined.

MANHATTAN GLAMOUR

Every home has a story to tell. This seven-story Beaux-Arts town house provided us the opportunity to elevate a phoenix from the ashes, really, after severe smoke and water damage from a neighboring house fire decimated the interiors its former owners had spent years reimagining and modernizing. The prospect of restoring the home again, while too much to bear for them, became an enticing prospect for our clients, who were looking for a home in New York City to accommodate their family, including rooms for their two young children, a chic entertaining floor, backyard, rooftop space, guest rooms, and above all else, a pool.

Having come from a more traditional setting, our clients were excited by the idea that their city dwelling would be decidedly urbane and glamorous. The home's sweeping, carved stone and glass staircase, and other contemporary architectural elements—remnants of the previous Gabellini Sheppard renovation that survived the fire—provided an ideal backdrop to create a stylish interior, including a new kitchen, dressing rooms, custom leather-clad library, and marble-wrapped spa. We carefully calibrated all our decorating choices to reincorporate a degree of tradition and ornament to bridge the gap between the building's nineteenth-century facade and its stark interiors.

We refinished many walls with quietly lavish materials, including polished plaster, onyx, alabaster, walnut, and shagreen, as well as five stories of fluted plaster in the stairwell, and luxurious upholstered walls in the media room and primary bedroom. We also completely reinvented

PAGE 2: Pairing a French gold lacquer screen from 1953 with Samuel Marx's matching lacquer cabinets from 1940 yields a high glamour quotient. PAGE 4: Mixing trend and tradition is key to our approach. OPPOSITE: The entry makes a statement about the push and pull of ornament in terms of history and modernity.

a few spaces—specifically the kitchen and the adjacent backyard—destroyed in the fire. The kitchen, our starting point, helped set the tone for how we thought about the rest of the house. Lining the kitchen cabinet interiors with vibrant colored leather—orange is the clients' favorite; it pops up throughout—made the point that we could design for longevity and add freshness and style with art, fabric, and details. We also transformed the roof to create a furnished backyard in the sky.

The living room set a stage for a play of the subtle and the eye-catching. Here, we employed luxe textiles, velvets, and silks to soften bolder statements made by the fixtures, embroideries, and metallic mantelpieces. The French art deco panel felt uniquely appropriate to command the sofa wall. Reminiscent of a scenic paper in its detail, it also added intrigue, a little history, and forged a connection to nearby Central Park.

In the dining room, we leveled up the drama. The custom table, inspired by an antique, introduced an element of tradition but is scaled to accommodate large groups. Contemporary chairs, covered in a sumptuous, cut-velvet Fortuny cloth, offset the reference to history; a few Midas touches of gold for artistry and enhancement gave the room the desired flourish, including the vintage 1970s gilded-bronze and rock-crystal candelabras originally cast for Cartier in Paris. The media room became its own realm of enjoyable luxury, a quietly opulent cocoon of plush cashmere, velvet, and parchment.

We felt the primary bedroom should be soft, warm, and quiet. Walls upholstered in a handwoven fabric provided a sumptuously restrained background for lacquered bedside tables, a custom leather bed, mid-century Italian lighting, and a deco carpet.

OPPOSITE: Venetian plaster and fluted walls balance the sleek contemporary stair with touches of tradition. FOLLOWING SPREAD: Luxurious contemporary seating, soigné vintage pieces, bejeweled vases, and gold accents, including Yves Klein's *Table Monogold,* create a potent, ultrachic mix in this living room. Custom embroidery on the curtain's leading edge offers a quiet response to the stair.

No matter how it's wrapped, framed, and decorated, a hearth always becomes a room's heart and soul—and its center of gravity—because it embodies the traditional notion of a gathering place.

The library provides the yin to the yang of the ethereal bedroom at the opposite end of the hall. Walnut with leather inset paneling trimmed in nickel and a mid-century rosewood desk created the decidedly handsome ambience, with some antiquity underfoot in a period rug.

For the children's rooms, we took great care to ensure that equity prevailed, with hopes to keep sibling rivalry to a minimum. Though the boys are not twins, we designed twinning rooms, almost inversions of one another in plan. In one, we opted for blue lacquer accents; in the other, green—their favorite colors. We leveled the playing field by enveloping both rooms with the same carpet, wall covering, and window treatments.

We combined two small rooms on the top floor to create a charming guest room under the eaves. Decoratively painted walls with an organic geode pattern provide a tranquil backdrop for the suite, and a plush patterned carpet created a serene, welcoming space for visiting family and friends.

We made sure throughout that every contemporary element was softened with touches of tradition and playfulness. In the end, the design emerged through choices—as it always does.

OPPOSITE: The custom metal bolection mantelpiece by Amuneal balances the glitter of the Damien Hirst work with a soft patina. The sconces by Roberto Giulio Rida are functional jewelry. PAGE 18: The bespoke parchment and gilded-brass console makes ornament practical. Cast plaster lamps that illuminate artwork by Mary Corse resonate with the stair's fluting. PAGE 19: The chairs' brass sabots play nicely with the custom chandelier. Gilt-bronze and rock-crystal table pieces created for Cartier by Claude Boeltz in the 1970s add the dazzle.

ABOVE: Hand-painted paper sheathes the powder room in a muted glow; Robert Motherwell's *Samurai II*, 1980, hangs on the wall. OPPOSITE: All the public spaces elevate glamour to its maximum chicness, each in its own way. The bar's custom antiqued brass mesh, slabs of Portoro gold stone, and bronze take their style cues from the adjacent formal dining room.

ABOVE: The kitchen encapsulates this home's design DNA. OPPOSITE: The space functions seamlessly, distinctively, and joyfully. We designed the ceiling fixtures, which are now part of our collection for Visual Comfort & Co. PAGE 24: The clients' orange crush features in high-impact moments like leather-lined upper cabinets. PAGE 25: The banquette's indoor/outdoor fabric folds in another citrus shade. The art is by Damien Hirst.

RIGHT: The media room's fabric-paneled walls conceal all the AV components. Dressed in Loro Piana cashmere, the sectional offers ultimate comfort. We designed the wool and linen rug, which is now in our collection with Loloi. The custom embroidery on the curtain's leading edge plays with abstraction. The artwork is by Hank Willis Thomas. PAGE 28, CLOCKWISE FROM TOP LEFT: Handmade lamps from Best & Lloyd provide glamorous accents with allusions to decorative history. A handcrafted leather chair with a hand-forged iron base amplifies the room's artisanal focus. The 1970s lizard and brass games table by Karl Springer introduces more skins into the room's exotic materials game, in which Todd Merrill's luminous, made-to-order goatskin table plays a major part. PAGE 29: Every room gains character through its specific mix of vintage, antique, and new pieces.

OPPOSITE AND ABOVE: The primary bedroom becomes a serene retreat with walls upholstered in a handwoven fabric from Nantucket Looms. Custom-designed bed linens echo Michel Contessa's chandelier. PAGE 32, CLOCKWISE FROM TOP LEFT: The fabric's plaid diffuses in daylight. A 1980s Garouste & Bonetti resin side table enhances the material complexity. A velvet ottoman offers plushness. Marie Suri's fire screen inserts whimsy with function. PAGE 33: A Samarkand Khotan rug lays a grounding of tradition.

ABOVE: The feminine dressing room is all elegance with lacquer and polished nickel finishes. The custom hardware from Matthew Studios incorporates rock crystal, which is a recurring motif throughout. OPPOSITE: Tommi Parzinger's nickel-finished candelabra sconces soften the minimalist primary bath. The artwork is by Damien Hirst.

OPPOSITE: With a nineteenth-century Persian Sultanabad carpet, inset leather-paneled walls, and a mid-century wing-chair, the library veers toward a more traditional taste.
ABOVE: Curtain fabric from Christopher Farr, a flame-stitch-covered lounge chair, and an updated take on a Chesterfield sofa amplify the pattern play.

OPPOSITE: A fraternal color-blocking story differentiates the boys' rooms. Durable faux suede upholsters the trundle beds. ABOVE: A pass-through connects the rooms. PAGES 40 AND 41: Each boy has his own Italian 1970s robot lamp, lacquered closet, and two-tone lounge and desk chairs. Splatter wallpaper and rainbow rugs tie the rooms together. Vibrant lacquered closet interiors make getting dressed a joy.

ABOVE: This guest bedroom under the eaves includes all the comforts of home.
OPPOSITE: Hand-applied plaster envelops the space in subtle pattern; the framed prints are from our collection with Soicher Marin. PAGE 44: Orange splashes enliven the pool lounge. PAGE 45: Vintage rattan seating offers easy poolside perches. PAGES 46–47: The furnished rooftop garden is such a New York story; the fountain recalls the house's Beaux-Arts facade.

BROOKLYN
BROWNSTONE

We believe that each phase of life comes with its own design needs, and sometimes true design imperatives. A budding, extremely stylish family like this one, for instance, generally tries to avoid anything that's too precious or that could be easily destroyed by a rambunctious yellow lab and three youngsters. Yet they still want a home that's chic, colorful, and completely hip. What's fun about this paradigm is that it calls on us to be very creative in specific, strategic ways. Every choice needs to be durable and practical. The mix of high and low, of aspirational and attainable, must meet the clients' vision and lifestyle. Often there's a desire to reincorporate pieces from a former residence into the new context, which means seeing how certain pieces can translate and have new life in the new rooms. Since we'd designed their previous home, we immediately keyed in on the pieces to bring along for the interiors of this Brooklyn brownstone, which they had commissioned a team of architects from The Brooklyn Studio to convert from a multifamily dwelling back to a single-family home.

We made sure the living room was chic, cheerful, and practical, not a precious space where children were not allowed. An approachable Chesterfield sofa, vibrant carpet, and stylish but simple linen curtain panels balanced the velvet-covered Bridgewater sofa and a postmodern-inspired coffee table. The vintage Eero Saarinen stools, re-covered with remnants of antique carpets, the light fixtures, and the artwork elevated the mix.

OPPOSITE: The nineteenth-century French gilt mirror adds luster and history. A high, low, and layered mix gives the living room its everyday chic, as well as the durability family living requires. FOLLOWING SPREAD: Linen, velvet, antique kilims, and tribal pillows create a rich yet light textural palette beneath a fixture from Visual Comfort & Co.

ABOVE: The color blue threads through the entire interior. The Robert Crowder wallpaper that gives the powder room its timely groove ties it together color-wise with the adjacent library. OPPOSITE: The library's bold blue lacquer reinforces the way the room connects the living and dining rooms, an arrangement that allows for easy flow when entertaining.

ABOVE: A well-stocked bar in the library turns this multiuse space into a hub for entertaining. A reflective wallpaper from Calico elevates bold pattern overhead. OPPOSITE: The sofa's coral silk-velvet upholstery lusciously balances the equally saturated but cool-toned walls. FOLLOWING SPREAD: A de Gournay wallpaper turns the dining room into an interior garden.

RIGHT: Our collaboration with The Brooklyn Studio included selecting the Farrow & Ball soft green paint that establishes the atmosphere of this glamorous kitchen. Pendants by The Urban Electric Co., the Calacatta gold marble that tops the kitchen island, and carefully chosen hardware introduce quiet notes of gleam that animate the cabinets.

We lacquered the library in the clients' favorite color, a rich shade of blue that threads through the parlor floor from one end to the other, and from the living room to the powder room, kitchen, and breakfast room. The pink settee and the sculpted rug that add such unexpected style to the library were another variation in the mix of high and low. Because the clients entertain frequently, we made sure that the smaller pieces of furniture were easily movable, and that traffic could flow organically through the parlor floor when the house is full of guests. The dining room's hand-painted wall covering, which ties into the garden, added another splurge of traditional decorative artistry to contrast with the sleek, functional modern dining table and chairs.

The entire second floor became the primary suite with a large bedroom, capacious walk-in closet, enormous bathroom, and an office. The third floor became the children's zone. In their son's room, we painted the interiors of the built-in bunk beds a sharp, dark royal blue, and wrapped the room in a paint splatter paper. At the time we were designing the house, they were expecting their third child, so we created a nursery with a cozy daybed fitted into the window for convenience and late nights. The nursery is adjacent to their daughter's bedroom, with foresight to potentially combine the two smaller bedrooms into one larger shared room for the girls when they're ready. One flight up, on the top floor, we created a playful multipurpose room, painted with circus stripes, that serves as a play area and a media room with built-in L-shaped daybeds with trundles underneath so that when family or friends visit, the space can become a bunk room for sleepovers.

OPPOSITE: The cheery indoor/outdoor Sunbrella fabric that covers the breakfast nook's custom built-in banquette makes meals with small children easy and cleanup after the inevitable spills a snap. The interior's mix of textures continues here in a practical way. The thematic shade of blue works its way into the table base. The artwork is by Claire Rosen.

ABOVE: The primary bedroom is a serenely comfortable retreat enveloped in the shades of the sky. The artwork reflects the clients' love of, and confidence in, the contrast of high and low. The art here is by Natasha Law.
OPPOSITE: In the enormous primary bath, an artwork by Hugo Guinness introduces another view of nature.

ABOVE: With trundle beds below, the velvet-covered daybeds allow the media room to double as a crash pad for visiting cousins and playmates. OPPOSITE: Smart in blue and white, the son's room feels boyish and fresh. PAGE 66: The nursery's window daybed permits easy transitions to and from the crib. PAGE 67: The daughter's bedroom, in a timeless palette, offers room to grow from princess to tween.

CALIFORNIA
DREAMING

t's always a privilege to help clients shape their homes to fit their evolving lifestyles, tastes, and families. It speaks to another level of trust when the relationship continues after a move to the opposite coast, as it has with these longtime clients, whom we've worked with as they've grown from newlyweds into a family of five. They recently purchased a Mediterranean-style house in Southern California with a 1920s core that had been expanded and renovated by Steve Giannetti not long ago for the former homeowners. With Steve's help and intimate knowledge of the property, we embarked upon additional modifications and enhancements to finesse the spaces for this family and their style of living and entertaining.

The long central entry hall that doubles as a gallery set just the right tone of welcome. The clients brought artwork and a few pieces of furniture from New York. We tailored the mix with several new contemporary pieces, which complement both the architectural style of the house and reflect who our clients have become over time.

The gracious scale of the main living room enabled us to have fun with two seating groups that contrasted with one another yet added balance and function to the room. Leaning into their desire for a more contemporary vibe, we decided that Vladimir Kagan's iconic, jet-set-era curved sofa was a perfect fit here, and not only because of its scale. It also beautifully offset the more classic rectilinear sofa by the fireplace.

The dining room, a more internal room in the home, was also part of the original 1920s structure. It opened to a planted interior courtyard that serves as a light well. Here we harked back to the clients' longtime love of

OPPOSITE: The push and pull of refined and rustic, of classic and contemporary, of engineered and organic materials begins in the entry gallery and contributes much to this home's character. The sleek center table plays counterpoint to the custom daybed, with vintage sconces and the lantern adding grace notes.

ABOVE: The architecture always sets the tone for the interior. The emphasis on views and the indoor/outdoor lifestyle informed all our decorating decisions.
OPPOSITE: The entry gallery extends the entire width of the house. The lanterns and custom hall table help bring the long, lofty space into more human scale.

RIGHT: The living room's ample dimensions allow for two separate but equal seating groups that balance refined and rustic materials and play more contemporary forms off clearly classic shapes. The fireplace at one end provides a natural focal point; we switched out its Mission-style black terra-cotta with a clean, modern plaster surround. A painting by Dashiell Manley hangs above.

FOLLOWING SPREAD: The space's sweep sparked the use of Vladimir Kagan's iconic Serpentine sofa, dressed in bouclé, to talk texture to the handwoven jute rug and the beamed ceiling. The metal legs of this group's lounge chairs mimic the armature of the overhead fixtures from Apparatus. Andrianna Shamaris's live-edge lychee wood coffee table and Adam Gale's hand-forged steel stools/side tables complexify the conversation of artisan-made elements. The artwork in the gallery is by Guillaume Linard Osorio.

PAGE 76: Forms, colors, and patterns recur at all levels of the space in various scales, materials, and textures. PAGE 77: The bases of the coffee tables bring details from overhead back down to earth. Rose Tarlow's side tables add a more delicate perspective on tree trunks into the room. ABOVE: The floral wall covering, which we designed for our collection with Lee Jofa, harks back to the wife's love of traditional decoration. OPPOSITE: A custom rift-oak table, contemporary dining chairs, and a favorite lighting fixture from the family's New York loft keep the room planted in the twenty-first century.

RIGHT: Because the family room connects to both the interior and exterior dining rooms, all the choices here reinforce those relationships visually. The grass cloth wall covering that envelops the room in subtle texture ties nicely to the lanterns that hover, nest-like, over the outdoor dining table. The lounge chair and ottoman by Harvey Probber meet the room's scale with a mid-century vibe that the sculptural tile-topped coffee table by Roger Capron enhances.

ABOVE: Nestled in the corner, the custom brass-topped bar invites people to gather or simply pick up a drink before heading outside. OPPOSITE: The sofa and bar relate through the echoing geometries of the sofa frame and the bar's paneling detail; their shared saturated blue anchors the room. FOLLOWING SPREAD: The terrace serves as the family's primary dining room.

RIGHT: With open space, expansive counters, abundant natural light, and a direct connection to the outdoors, this kitchen embodies the California ideal for these transplanted New Yorkers. The vintage pendant light and the contemporary stools add contrasting patinas.

FOLLOWING SPREAD: The vintage/modern mix takes on a different flavor in the breakfast area where the dining table from the family's former residence found new life. The chairs are mid-twentieth-century favorites by Osvaldo Borsani.

RIGHT: Serenity reigns in the primary bedroom, an oasis upstairs that's nested amid the treetops. An antique rug floats like a cloud underfoot. FOLLOWING SPREAD: The wife's love of soft, romantic florals blooms again in the sitting area of the primary bedroom. The 1970s-style coffee table is a piece we acquired for their first apartment that has lived happily in every one of their homes since.

pretty florals with a patterned wall covering and countered that touch of tradition with contemporary furnishings, including a light fixture brought along from their former SoHo loft.

The family room, which opens to the outdoor dining room, became a key part of the entertaining hub with the incorporation of a brass-topped bar. The clients, wine enthusiasts, loved the idea of a functioning bar with a sweeping counter for guests to gather around during parties large and small. Here, we developed a flexible furniture plan that allowed for both gracious entertaining and circulation among adjoining spaces, inside and out.

The existing kitchen was the ideal for transplanted New Yorkers: light, bright, open to the vegetable gardens and outdoor pizza oven and grilling station, and expansive enough that we were able to include the dining table and chairs from their SoHo loft. It was fun for us to revisit these pieces that were perfect for different reasons in other situations and repurpose them to take on a whole new look and life.

The primary suite upstairs took on the feel of a tree house with its glass expanses. The floral patterns and more traditional upholstered pieces here stemmed back to their first New York apartment, our initial project with them. The 1970s coffee table found many moons ago came from that apartment; it's one of several pieces from our beginnings together that have endured from home to home.

We transformed the former media room into a luxurious screening room with upholstered walls and two tiers of sofas so all ages could sit together comfortably when watching movies. Here, as elsewhere, the unexpected mix of materials and interesting juxtapositions of forms provide visual impact and excitement. Yet, as throughout, we've balanced the visual with the practical, ensuring that, above all, the room's function and purpose are intact.

OPPOSITE: When opportunity permits, there is probably no greater luxury than a primary bath with a fabulous view like this one. Placing the tub in the window bay maximizes the rare parental moments of respite by making the most of the garden vistas. Vaughan's ethereal ceiling fixture descends like a shimmering waterfall.

ABOVE: The children's playroom opens conveniently off their rooms.
OPPOSITE: Color blocking, pattern play, and a mix of textures create a fun, cheerful atmosphere that feels just right for the kids' bedrooms.

Part of the process is coming up with unexpected solutions to everyday decorating challenges, such as how best to hang an important piece of art. A patterned and upholstered wall covered in cut-velvet fabric is hardly ever the first thought, but it may be the best thought for seeing the artwork in a new light.

PREVIOUS SPREAD: The screening room takes the high-low mix to another level. Walls upholstered in a cut-velvet fabric from Brunschwig & Fils bring the chic with acoustic benefits. Modular instead of theater-style seating means the family can hang out together comfortably by themselves or with friends. And if the children want to sprawl together or climb from one sofa to the next, they can. The artwork is by Carrier and Company for Soicher Marin.
OPPOSITE: Artwork by Frankie Tobin pops brilliantly off the patterned wall covering.

ABOVE: All pathways lead to the central courtyard, creating gorgeous views in every direction. OPPOSITE: The indoor/outdoor lifestyle that makes Southern California so special played a key role in every design decision. In this house, the interior rooms unfold to the exterior spaces seamlessly. Some key decorative motifs from the living room reappear in the adjacent furnished loggia, underscoring the connection.

ABOVE: All pathways lead to the central courtyard, creating gorgeous views in every direction. OPPOSITE: The indoor/outdoor lifestyle that makes Southern California so special played a key role in every design decision. In this house, the interior rooms unfold to the exterior spaces seamlessly. Some key decorative motifs from the living room reappear in the adjacent furnished loggia, underscoring the connection.

CONTEMPORARY
LAKE HOUSE

As designers, we find few things more gratifying than when clients come back to us to help them realize a new project. This family had originally reached out to us when they decided to acquire and transform a dilapidated 1950s summer camp—an enormous main lodge and several little cabins—into guest quarters adjacent to their existing lakefront house in Connecticut. Several years later, after family and friends (and even our clients) admitted to preferring the spaces we'd created out of old cabins across the road to the lakefront home they'd grown up in, they decided to reenvision and refresh their lakefront house. We teamed with architect Jim Dixon to add expanses of glass and modernize the interiors just as we did with the cabins across the street.

The existing shingle-style house was narrow, compartmentalized, and quite traditional. Avid art collectors, our clients dreamed of creating a loft on the lake within the house's more traditional confines. They also asked for plenty of wall space to rotate the works from their collection. We were able to refresh the house into a much more forward leaning, progressive home by adding spans of glass that celebrated the views and reconfiguring the flow and floor plan to shape interiors that felt more expansive and connected. We took down all the non-supporting walls and removed door frames to make the spaces as open and connected as possible, as well as more accommodating to the pieces in their art collection. The one structural wall we could not remove, we clad in wood for contrast and warmth and created a focal point and backdrop for more artwork, turning a negative into a positive.

OPPOSITE: In the main stair hall, reimagined with James Dixon Architect, Olafur Eliasson's light sculpture, a Hilary Pecis painting, and a Deborah Roberts' work on paper make the opening statement. FOLLOWING SPREAD: The living room, dressed in neutrals, lets Petrit Halilaj's installation command center stage above the custom limestone mantel. Danish lounge chairs provide an elegant mid-century contrast.

Before we started, the client admitted they rarely used the living room because it felt far away and totally detached from the rest of the house. Reinventing the entry to the space created a sense of invitation and opened it up to the rest of the interior. We were able to create back-to-back seating areas due to the length and depth of the room's dimensions; one encompasses the view of the lake; the other addresses the fireplace. Now architecturally engaged with the rest of the home, and furnished with a Scandinavian-inspired rug, Danish mid-century chairs, and simple sheer curtains, a room that was once rarely used is the most coveted. For the TV room—an evening room they retire to when they want a change of view—we shifted to a slightly darker, more saturated, but still quite neutral palette, with grass cloth on the walls to add some understated texture and create an alternative backdrop for their very contemporary artwork. The family room, just up the steps, we centered on the existing fireplace. The renovation connected it organically to the kitchen, a dining area with a Saarinen table and rattan chairs, steps away from the porch they use as their plein air dining room.

The lower level had been a warren of storage rooms, guest rooms, a billiards room, and an office. We took this opportunity to reorganize the plans to leverage the lakeside views, removing unnecessary partitions, and adding a glazed partition to bring in as much natural light as possible into the core of the space. As we reimagined it, this open, flowing interior has shifted its focus to stylish spaces that emphasize the captivating views—those made by man and by nature.

OPPOSITE: A Hugo McCloud work infuses color into the living room's second seating area. A custom rug ties the room together. FOLLOWING SPREAD: In this fully transformed home, only the family room's stone lintel and fireplace remain from the house's previous iteration. Woven chairs around the dining area's Eero Saarinen table balance David Gordon's painting.

RIGHT: The kitchen now functions as a convenient hub for the family room, interior dining room, and exterior dining porch. The room's well-windowed walls nixed the usual upper cabinet configuration, prompting us to incorporate as much storage area as possible into the central island. Framed in the same oak, the built-in china cabinet maximizes function with a modern point of view.

RIGHT: The neutral palette in the media room swerves into saturated, dark tones for a change of mood—and because the family tends to use the space at night. Grass cloth wall covering imbues the walls with subtle texture that provides a wonderful backdrop for bold works of art. Understated patterns in the rug and the curtain panels at the window, plus throw pillows in different textures and colors, provide just the right amount of contrast for balance. The painting is by Till Freiwald.

It's incredibly important to give each room in the house its own distinctive identity. It's just as important to make sure that the spirit, character, and quality of the decoration is cohesive throughout. The goal is individuality with overall consistency.

OPPOSITE: Textural play gives the media room much of its personality. FOLLOWING SPREAD: A seating area outside the office creates another opportunity for conversations and contemplation. Again, the neutral palette lets the art charge and color the atmosphere. Throw pillows connect to the art by Hank Willis Thomas above the sofa; the sculpture is by Otani Workshop. PAGES 120-21: On this screened porch, the outdoor furnishings are an extension of the interior's overall style and ethos.

HISTORIC TUDOR

Because we see design as a balancing act, finding the happy medium for a family with different points of view is always an interesting and often rewarding challenge. In renovating this 1920s Tudor house to meet their family's needs and lifestyle, our clients set out to double the square footage of the home so meticulously that it is hard to tell what is and isn't original. The husband, a fan of traditional decorating, loved the original house's existing dark oak-paneled interiors and period details. The wife, who'd worked in some of New York's premier modern art galleries, preferred lighter, more colorful spaces. To create the blend, we selected many furnishings with traditional shapes and forms, then enlivened them with brighter, bolder colors and patterns that make an impact throughout. We also happily incorporated and kept intact some of the decorative elements from the original Tudor decor, such as the living room's silver-plated sconces and limestone mantelpiece.

The entry foyer with its modern white center table, tufted settee, and contemporary art became the prelude to the mix. The sunken living room we left as we found it, just reconditioned the paneling. We had fun with the pieces, choosing antiques like a nineteenth-century wing chair and Chippendale chair that felt modern because of their unexpectedly large scale and their neighbors, in this case a contemporary, mirror-topped, red-leather-clad coffee table. In contrast with the traditional velvet English roll arm sofa, graphic fabrics and bright trims inserted a sense of modernity and freshness, especially set atop a light but traditionally patterned Oushak carpet.

Our clients wanted the ability to host holidays and events for their large, extended family. With this in mind, they needed a dining room that could accommodate their immediate family of six but could also comfortably seat twenty at one table for the holidays. The renovation doubled the scale of the original

OPPOSITE: The foyer's mix of elements introduces the happy medium between the house's dominant Tudor vocabulary and its more playful contemporary colors, patterns, and forms. The chandelier and silvered wallpaper with a stripe motif of stylized vines nod to the traditional, while the lacquered center table injects the now. The artwork is by Natasha Law.

dining room, so we designed a custom table that consists of a pair of square-top dining tables, which we centered under the lanterns, to make the space intimate enough for every day. With a third drop-leaf table, contained below the skirted serving table, the two square tables convert to one enormous banquette table.

The butler's pantry was organized to tie the dining room to the new wing with a double-height family room, enormous kitchen, guest room, and primary bedroom suite. With a wallpaper on the ceiling here, we pulled in some of the blue that weaves through the house.

The paneled library, part of the original Tudor, remained intact with its beautifully leaded windows and walnut paneling. The cozy scale of this room, in addition to its prime location between the formal entry and family breakfast room, made it an ideal music room.

Architecturally, we took some liberties in the kitchen, part of the new wing, by bleaching the oak beams to make them less baronial. We also blended materials: contrasting painted cabinets and quartzite countertops around the perimeter with the marble-topped wooden island. The double-height family room, just opposite, is open to the kitchen and where the family can gather casually to play a game or watch TV. Here, though we embraced all the traditional details, we dialed up the color, contrast, and patterns, and considered more durable fabrics and finishes that will endure the wear and tear that comes with raising a family.

For the primary suite upstairs, we shifted the balance again, folding in even more contemporary elements to enliven both the antechamber that serves as an office/sitting room/TV room and the bedroom behind it. We dovetailed the two together with the same window treatments, and a unified color scheme.

Having achieved a delicate and seamless balance between its original traditional twentieth-century roots and the twenty-first-century addition required to serve the needs of busy, modern family life, this home feels both fresh and familiar, as timeless as it is stylish.

OPPOSITE: The foyer steps down into the living room, which retains its original Tudor gravitas thanks to the now reconditioned oak paneling and ceiling beams. With the foyer's settee, the living room's mohair-dressed, traditional English roll arm sofa with understated tape trim brings one of the interior's dominant color motifs into focus. The artwork over the mantel is by Thomas Libetti.

RIGHT: Traditional shapes and forms enlivened with bright, bold colors and patterns make an impact within the dark oak surroundings. Scale also plays a significant role in this drama of now and then. The oversize antique Chippendale chair stands out in its updated lacquer finish. Artwork flanking the doorway is by Neal Perbix. PAGE 128: The contemporary Oushak rug puts down a period foundation. An oversize nineteenth-century wood-frame wingback chair upholstered in a contemporary Brunschwig & Fils pattern also brings the traditional into the twenty-first century. Even the curtains express this push-pull. PAGE 129, CLOCKWISE FROM UPPER LEFT: The color motifs tie disparate patterns together. Reconditioned woodwork and original hardware bring a wonderful patina. A specimen marble table inserts a joyful burst of color. Ethnic fabrics offer the shock of the new; the red tape and nail-head trim adds spice.

ABOVE: Brightened with a lacquer finish, new paneling in the dining room references the interior's original Tudor detailing. OPPOSITE: In the expanded dining room, two custom dining tables sit beneath the lanterns; the roll-out centerpiece with pop-up leaves that connects them into a banquet-sized table lives under the skirted side table. Raffia wallpaper introduces another layer of pattern and texture. The art is by Leah Durner.

ABOVE: In shades of green, the powder room off the foyer brings the wooded exterior inside. OPPOSITE: In the butler's pantry, a marbleized paper carries some of the dining room's blue overhead and softens the traditional millwork. FOLLOWING SPREAD: The house's original mahogany-paneled library now doubles as a music room and connects the foyer to the breakfast room.

RIGHT: The breakfast room has remained intact, from its leaded-glass windows to its moldings. All the furnishings recall classic models. The host chair, an updated take on a wing chair, clearly speaks to tradition with a contemporary twist. FOLLOWING SPREAD: Though the ceiling beams and other elements of the new kitchen embrace the house's Tudor origins, the lighter finishes are in keeping with the addition's twenty-first-century heritage. The checkerboard backsplash of glazed terra-cotta tiles also walks the line of past and present: the tiles are an ancient material, yet here they nod to the graphic pop of some prints used throughout. The mix of materials—painted cabinets versus the stone-topped wood island versus the Caesarstone on the perimeter countertops for daily use—prioritizes utility, and aesthetics equally.

Balancing tradition with modernity is an ongoing design challenge, and always so interesting because the solution evolves out of each location, architectural context, and family lifestyle. The right fun, unexpected pops of color and graphic pattern can do so much to make a historic house more youthful, bright, and cheerful.

OPPOSITE: The double-height family room that unfolds off the kitchen is the space where everyone gathers. The panel detail here replicates the original elsewhere; painted white, and combined with the vibrant yellow walls above, it makes the room glow. The curtain panels drop columns of cheerful, bold pattern around the room. The custom wool and silk rug adds modernity to the room with the stripe, and not just in color but in ribs of cut pile and flat weave.

RIGHT: Covered in Crypton-finished velvet, the sofas look their best while supporting all sorts of family fun. The leaded-glass doors behind the sofa open to the outdoor dining area. The texture story continues in the Moroccan-inspired pattern of the cut-pile fabric on the wood armchairs, a Carrier and Company design for Century Furniture. A large custom ottoman with an inset tray holds the center of this seating arrangement. The artwork pairs contemporary abstraction with vintage organic for contrast and playfulness.

PAGE 144: Antique iron bistro tables with white glass tops flank the sofas, bringing a patina of age into the mix and commenting interestingly on the contemporary polished concrete and hand-forged iron occasional tables.

PAGE 145: Stripes of all different kinds and colors play an integral role in this interior's pattern language.

ABOVE: Our Morgan chair, covered in velvet and detailed with a linen cord, pulls up to our Frederick writing table in the primary bedroom's sitting area. OPPOSITE: Mirrored nightstands bring moments of glamour into the primary bedroom. PAGE 148: A vibrant burst of color adds to the suite's mix. The artwork is by Mary Nelson Sinclair. PAGE 149: The primary bedroom's geometric and floral forms and patterns dovetail harmoniously.

ABOVE: The sunroom includes a bar for convenience when entertaining. OPPOSITE: Adjacent to the pool and outdoor dining venue, this room doubles as a luncheon spot and, during the summer, a pool house. The deep blue tile underfoot provides a pop of color around the perimeter. FOLLOWING SPREAD: Teak chaise longues overlook the pool and formal garden.

ACT I

Most clients dream of creating a perfect stage set for the backdrop of their urban lives. Jessica Chastain, the award-winning actor and producer, found hers and her now husband's in a landmarked nineteenth-century building near Central Park. The apartment, all mirrored 1970s glam at the time of purchase, came with fabulous bones. It also had an illustrious provenance, given previous tenants that included Adam Guettel, Bobby Short, and Leonard Bernstein, a lineage fit for someone who loves the performing arts as much as Jessica does.

She was enamored with the building's charm, which oozed from the surviving vestiges of the original architecture: mahogany paneling, elaborately carved doorways and windows, plaster crown moldings, and oak parquet floors. Stripping off the mirror and decades of paint and paper, we discovered that every room had, or at one point had, a fireplace. The building had a long-standing practice of archiving architectural artifacts designated for discard during renovations; we scoured this incredible resource for fireplace parts and mantels when we began to reconstitute the rooms.

The atmosphere for each room emerged from a fantasy based partly on Jessica's passion for theater and love of the Golden Age of Hollywood, and partly on her own decidedly romantic vision.

The parlor already had mood, depth, and darkness with stained-glass windows and their mahogany casings. It didn't make sense to do anything bright or

OPPOSITE: The library doubles as a screening room and harks back to a certain era of New York City glamour with its silk wall covering, a cashmere-covered sofa, and the French mirror panels that conceal a TV. FOLLOWING SPREAD: In the living room, deep-green-saturated walls and sofa, a neoclassical gilt mirror, and lounge chairs recall the apartment's original period. The slipper chair belonged to Lauren Bacall. On the mantel are artworks by Thomas Libetti and George Condo. The majority of the furnishings, including furniture, fabrics, paint, lighting, and floorcoverings, throughout are from Ralph Lauren Home except where noted.

Historic architecture always presents the push-pull of the past and present, and the challenge of calibrating the best possible balance between the two. It's incredibly gratifying to breathe new life, glamour, and sophistication into spaces that retain strong vestiges of their origins.

white here, so we wrapped the room in tea-stained floral linen, mixed in a vintage chandelier we relocated from a back room, and created an office. The adjacent living room took on more saturation with decoratively painted dark green sueded walls, an antique mirror, and a little chintz chair that once belonged to Lauren Bacall. We amplified the romance in the primary suite with an in-room bathtub inspired by London's Dean Street Townhouse, one of Jessica's favorite places. For the library, we went ultraluxe with cashmere on the sofa, velvet on the chairs, and silk on the walls. We designed custom millwork here to conceal an eighty-inch screen above the fireplace, so the room doubles as Jessica's private screening room.

Piece by piece, room by room, this apartment evolved, and eventually the dream became a reality, and the house became home.

OPPOSITE: The parlor, like so much of the rest of this interior, is informed by history thanks to the surviving original woodwork and stained glass and leaded windows. A custom mantel respectfully introduces a touch of the now. The subtle grid of the cloth wall covering installation takes its cues from the fenestration details. Discovered elsewhere in the apartment, the vintage chandelier adds a needed touch of eccentricity—and so much charm.

ABOVE: The kitchen feels like the room in the apartment that is most indebted to its origins just because of the architecture of its framework. Given the ceiling height, the rolling ladder makes great practical sense. RIGHT: We designed and added the custom central island to provide a pop of color and practicality.

OPPOSITE: Challenge made, challenge met with the engineering and installation of the copper pedestal tub within the primary bedroom itself. The paintings are by Jacques Nestlé. The chair is vintage. ABOVE: The curtained canopy bed from Ralph Lauren speaks to Jessica's romance with decoration. The antique nineteenth-century rug brings in the patina that comes only with age.

LANDMARKED LUXURY

Our approach to design tends to involve finding just the right calculus of tradition and modernity for the client and the location. These homeowners, a young family of four, combined two units in one of Manhattan's storied, turn-of-the-century courtyard apartment buildings, a vintage and style they adored. While they wished to keep the scale and sense of architecture appropriate to what it would have originally been, they favored a loftlike open plan with a large, stylish kitchen that connected to the dining and living areas. We worked with architect Gordon Kahn to realize their goals.

This family loves to travel and has accumulated many mementos from their trips, including numerous works of art that we framed and incorporated throughout. These personal artifacts influenced our decisions during the design process. We worked to find pieces that heightened the effect of each work of art and at the same time elevated the entire grouping into a harmonious composition with a balance of materials, styles, and periods.

We developed an easy, open, somewhat esoteric floor plan for the living area that met their entertaining needs and the quirks of the space. It made sense to pull together different periods, styles, textures, and countries of origin in a mélange of furnishings that reflected the family's interests and travels. Because the living area was more trapezoid than rectangle, we designed a curved sofa to wrap around the odd angles and invite people into the space. We also had the carpet, with its art deco-inspired border, woven to fit the unique angles of the floor plan.

OPPOSITE: The reintroduction of architectural detail, which begins in the entry foyer, balances this residence's loftlike open plan. The custom-made wood, metal, and glass console evokes history with contemporary materials. FOLLOWING SPREAD: The living room reflects this family of travel lovers in its mélange of styles, periods, and countries of origin. For entertaining, the furniture placement encourages easy traffic flow.

ABOVE: Nesting tables in shagreen and bronze echo the curve of the sofa and add to the room's exoticism. OPPOSITE: Displaying collected treasures to their best advantage—like this large painting brought back from a monastery in Bhutan—means creating settings that allow them to stand out while also contributing to the mix. The sideboard is by Tommi Parzinger.

From the entry to the inner rooms, we played with the contrast of dark and light. The pale polished plaster in the public areas—including the dining area with its extension table—gave way to a moody dark green grass cloth wall covering in the family room to create a cozy, intimate space for family game night or watching a show. Green is a favorite color of theirs. It became this room's recurring theme in the faux malachite-painted games table, on the velvet-covered sofa, custom wool carpet, and the chair and a half, which they use to cuddle up and read with their children.

Because the kitchen was at one end of the space and open to the living room at the other, it had to be just as beautifully appointed. Its moldings, hand-painted millwork, and warm brown oak accents—all part and parcel of the architecture—served to tie it organically to the spaces immediately adjacent.

With its red-leather-lined bookcases, the lacquered library was designed to accommodate many different uses. The space had to work as a his-and-hers office by day and the homework room after school with a pair of built-in desks. A custom sleeper sofa was employed to allow for extra guests when needed; the mirror TV over the mantelpiece made the space also function as a second media room.

Our vision for the primary bedroom was to create a peaceful sanctuary with a soft French blue glaze on paneled walls and matching silk curtain panels to envelope the room. A contemporary sleigh bed and a chair with cast bronze legs, a mid-century Italian light fixture, and ivory leather-wrapped bedside chests added balance and light to the room's serenity.

The mix of styles, materials, and periods, the contrast of light and dark elements, the inclusion of favorite pieces collected on family travels—all are fundamental factors that contribute to the style and allure of this family home.

OPPOSITE: The beam placement and rhythm of the ceiling coffering inform the layout of the dining and living areas within the expansive open space. The dining room table seats eight for every day, and more with leaves that extend it for holidays and other celebrations.

PRECEDING SPREAD: The clients favor green; we opted for the "more is more" approach with it in the media room. The artwork with painted-over film strips is a little tongue in cheek. ABOVE LEFT: The vintage Karl Springer games table layers in another green. ABOVE RIGHT: So does the custom wool carpet. OPPOSITE: And the upholstery on the chair and a half.

RIGHT: Because there is a professional chef in the family, we considered the kitchen's function as deeply as its form. With help from Christopher Peacock, the kitchen balances the two ends of the living space and is open to the living and dining areas, so it needed to be equally special from an aesthetic perspective. We used hand-painted surfaces rather than spray-lacquered ones, and devised moldings that splice together with those in the rest of the apartment. The rich brown oak of the island made sense because it tied into the floors and the doors and became part and parcel of the interior architecture.

RIGHT: The private study/
library, though smaller than
the public rooms, serves
a multitude of functions.
The two built-in desks
that, with bookcases, flank
the fireplace—perhaps
the last vestige of the
original interior—do double
duty as home offices
by day and homework
areas for the kids by night.
The sofa is a sleeper
for spillover. A mirror
TV over the mantelpiece
turns the space into
another media room.

ABOVE: The custom carpet takes color and pattern cues from the vintage kilim that covers the ottoman. OPPOSITE: With just the right players in just the right scale, a room's various elements dovetail seamlessly to support many different functions. The textural mix speaks intimately and warmly of comfort.

RIGHT: Drenched in a French blue glaze, wall paneling in the primary bedroom brings a sense of history and, just as important, an enhanced degree of visual order and intimacy. Adding silk curtain panels in a matching color creates a very ethereal effect. The French blue threads through the carpet pattern, the chair upholstery, and the most discrete little trim on the pleated silk lampshades. The sleigh bed, leather-clad bedside chests, and bronze chair legs balance the prettiness of the blue with a more modern presence; the choice of camel tones for contrast was inspired by the yellow brick of the apartment building across the street. Overhead is a mid-century Italian fixture.

CONTINENTAL
PIED-À-TERRE

L ife is never static, so interior style tends to evolve with lifestyle. Growing families present us with opportunities for spatial creativity and decoration, and empty nests do as well. This design-loving couple was in the process of transitioning from a house designed for a seven-person family to a new, smaller apartment with one child still at home. They purchased a wonderful pied-à-terre—a duplex jewel box in a great art deco building on Central Park—intending to create a residence that would suit their newfound lifestyle. With Tsao & McKown Architects, we set in motion plans to create an elegant and versatile home.

On the main floor, they asked for a gracious space to entertain large groups, copious wall area to display artworks, and intimate spaces for small gatherings. For the best of all worlds, we devised an open floor plan partitioned by a dividing wall. On one side, we created a colorful, quite contemporary family room. On the flip side, we made a more traditional, formal room with French bergères, a gilded coffee table, and a classic sofa. These two spaces can serve as one, dressed up and pared down at once.

The clients had seen a pair of brutalist metal doors within a traditional interior on an architectural tour of Italy, a memory that inspired the kitchen's pocket doors. The couple loved the idea of leaving an imprint on everything they touched, so we gave the kitchen's upper cabinets a nickel finish for a contemporary patina. The breakfast room's furnishings accentuated the overall blend by combining classic twentieth-century designs under a silver-leaf ceiling.

In the primary suite upstairs, timeless textiles blend with vestiges of their former home, including an antique highboy, one of their first purchases after they married.

The Italian and French references, and nods to different periods, gave this residence a continental feel that reflects the clients' spirit.

OPPOSITE: The neutral palette in the family room ensures that the art by Robert Mangold is the primary focus. The alpaca rug underlays the space with plush softness; the chenille sofa fabric keeps things cozy; silk and cashmere throw pillows inject spots of color that help make the space an inviting gathering place.

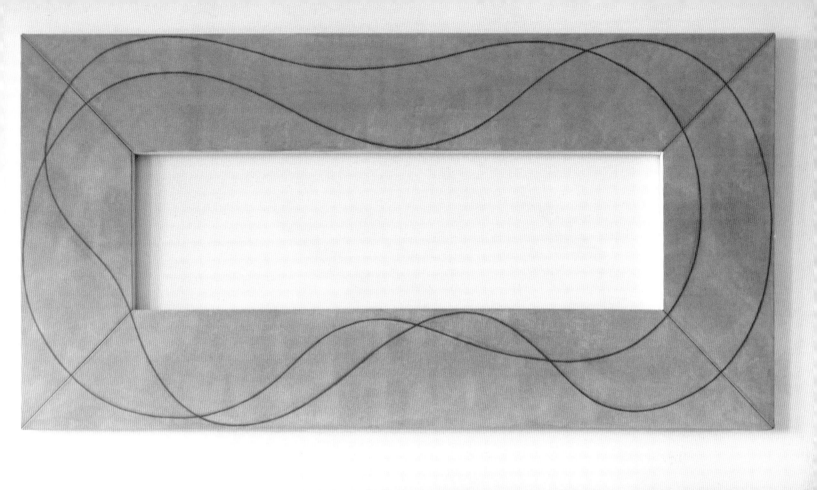

LEFT: The polished plaster walls that give the family room its glow continue through the living room, here wrapping the mantelpiece with a custom white bronze surround and subtly setting off flanking custom parchment cabinets by Daniel Scuderi. Incorporating some of the clients' existing pieces into their new home is almost always an objective. Here, these include the skirted split-back club chairs and a tufted-leather ottoman atop the hand-knotted, braided abaca rug by Doris Leslie Blau, which together speak to continuity, change, and above all, comfort in the formal living room. The artwork is by, from left to right, Yves Klein, Sigmar Polke, and Catherine Wagner. FOLLOWING SPREAD: In this apartment, the artwork becomes a part of the space and the architecture. The floating wall that separates the living and the family rooms offers a prime spot for artwork, here a painting by David Hockney. The living room answers the clients' desire for a more formal setting and flexibility for large-scale entertaining. The gilded brass and glass coffee table keeps the room light. The curves and carvings of antique Louis XVI bergères balance the angles of the room's more contemporary elements. A 1945 mahogany pedestal table and mahogany armchairs, both by Maison Leleu, create an elegant, intimate spot by the window for homework, games, or conversation.

ABOVE: For these clients, chic and practicality go hand in hand. The artwork is a light box by James Turrell. RIGHT: Pocket doors part like brutalist curtains to reveal the kitchen's patinated drama. Jean-Michel Frank dining chairs, circa 1930, surround a vintage Eero Saarinen dining table. The pendant light by C. J. Weinstein from the 1930s adds more luster.

ABOVE: The reconfigured upper floor houses this airy, light-filled primary bedroom. The custom four-poster bed is crafted of solid mahogany. Filled with sentimental value, the George III chest-on-chest is the first antique the clients purchased together decades ago. OPPOSITE: The updated primary bath takes advantage of the view. The antique stool interjects the vintage and hand-hewn into the crisp, contemporary surroundings.

LAKE HOUSE
LEGACY

Experience has taught us that each house, and every family, has its own unique story to tell of generational change. But this house—a center-hall colonial in Connecticut, built some twenty years ago as a weekend retreat for a family of three—was truly a first for us in terms of cross-generational attachment. The homeowners and their adult daughter, now herself a wife and mother, wanted the entire family to continue to connect here on weekends for the foreseeable future. Our goal, with architect Jim Dixon, was to craft the existing house into a cohesive two-family home under one roof. In other words, this one project encompassed two distinct clients with separate sets of needs and points of view.

The clients had lived in the house long enough to know what they wished to change about it. Their original open plan had worked well for years, but now separate, dedicated rooms made more sense. Except for the entrance and the kitchen, which we expanded significantly, we doubled just about every other type of room so that the two families could be together when they desired and be apart from each other gracefully.

Our approach has always been to make a home feel like it's been collected over the course of the homeowners' lives. Here, we had two distinct lifetimes to consider. To bridge the difference, we blended existing pieces throughout, including the great room's coffee table and armoire, with new introductions and vintage finds, including a set of 1940s-era Danish chairs.

OPPOSITE: In expanding and renovating this center-hall colonial, built two-plus decades ago as a weekend house, to accommodate the now multiple generations of their family—really, two families under a shared roof—these clients prioritized a plan that encouraged both privacy and community, made the most of the views, and embraced the property's beloved great old oaks and other precious trees.

To capture the lake views, the living room addition was oriented off the back of the house, and we repurposed the former library/formal living room as the formal dining room with its existing built-ins. Another wing was added to serve as a separate media room with a second primary suite above. We even rehabbed the attic into a playroom for the third generation.

The kitchen expansion tripled the room's original size. We designed a custom kitchen table that doubles as an island and customized the surrounding chairs to satisfy the height differences of the household members, who are, like the three bears in the classic story, very small, very tall, and in between. When selecting upholstery materials—a solid or geometric, but not floral, and in just the right shade of blue—every family member had an equally weighted vote, and only granted approval if all members agreed. When these clients had opinions, like their desire for a sectional sofa in the kitchen corner rather than the expected banquette and table, they were absolute.

For the primary suite on the ground floor, we made nominal changes, adding some wainscoting, removing some outdated built-ins, and washing all the surfaces in a pale Swedish blue. Upstairs, the same aesthetic came into play in what is now the second primary bedroom.

This project showed us once again that as individual as each generation of a family may be, they also resemble apples—and rarely fall far from the tree.

OPPOSITE: Light-filled and gracious, the foyer originally unfolded into the open-plan living areas that characterized the first floor of this house in its initial iteration. Newly enclosed in the renovation, it remains the primary point of entry.

RIGHT: An addition to the property, this living room on the ground floor is furnished for comfort first—and in such a way as to suggest that it has evolved over time. The antique Tabriz carpet from Galerie Shabab almost casually lays down a foundation of tradition atop a bound sisal area rug. The nail-head-studded club chairs and ottoman add to the timeless effect. The antique Swedish armoire is a happy holdover from the interior's early days.

LEFT: The renovation opened all rooms to the fabulous view. ABOVE: This living room now unfolds gracefully on to a new terrace. PAGE 202: A custom settee anchors a cozy living room seating area with a nineteenth-century French pedestal table and a set of 1940s Danish armchairs. PAGE 203: A mix of items from various eras creates an interior that feels collected over time.

As a family business, we genuinely understand the importance of family life, its evolution and the impact it makes on interior design decisions. We feel it's always important to remember and honor the truth that certain design decisions can and should correspond to and perfect the clients' vision of their lifestyle now and for the future.

OPPOSITE: The vastly expanded new kitchen centers on the island, a work space that does double duty as a multigenerational gathering area. FOLLOWING SPREAD: A sitting area in the windowed kitchen corner, instead of a breakfast table, allows for family to gather and enjoy the room all day. PAGE 208: Seating options abound in dining areas indoors and out. PAGE 209: Everyone celebrated the classic color palette of blue and white.

ABOVE AND OPPOSITE: The consistent color palette serves as the unifying thread that pulls the disparate spaces—including this butler's pantry, washed in a beautiful Swedish blue—into a cohesive whole. FOLLOWING SPREAD: With pairs of lounge chairs and end tables flanking the sofa, saturated in the deepest blue, the den's furniture plan optimizes the comfort of symmetry.

ABOVE AND OPPOSITE: The softest of blues and crispest of whites make this ground-floor primary suite a beguiling retreat. PAGE 216: The shiplap wainscot adds depth and texture to the primary bath. PAGE 217: The second-floor primary suite shares an aesthetic sensibility with the first.

When many voices come together in a complex project and all are focused on the same goals and a happy outcome, it really is true that teamwork makes the dream work.

OPPOSITE: The addition of a screened porch ample enough to accommodate living and dining areas was a key aspect of the expansion. The wicker pieces carry all the connotations that come with the idea of a classic country house and family retreat. The fabrics—again, solids and checks—tie the interior and exterior together.

ARTFUL IN THE HAMPTONS

Integrating artworks into the design of an interior sparks such interesting questions, which is why it's a thrill to have serious collectors like this New York couple for clients. With an inventory list of their collection in hand, our design process for this Hamptons estate began with the artwork. Given the unimpeded sight lines from room to room, we wanted to ensure that no one single piece or series overpowered the surroundings. Our goal was to balance materials, forms, colors, textures, and details—and above all, the art—to create cohesion.

The double-height entry, a crossroads of sorts, offered views into the living and dining rooms and upstairs. Here, we mixed rustic and refined, patina and polish, with a Giacometti-inspired center table, contemporary mobile-like chandelier, and an overscale verdigris mirror to hint at the clients' aesthetic sensibility.

The living room serves as a passageway, connecting the entry foyer to the family room, as well as to the garden. It is also where guests might gather for a cocktail before dinner. Our furniture plan therefore had to be centric, and the pieces had to be visually open, so guests could see through and navigate around them. Here, a backless daybed allows for guests to engage with others in the room or quietly gaze out at the garden beyond the French doors.

The dining room, in contrast, was distinctly an evening space. The clients, with a museum mentality, instinctively envisioned white walls. We suggested a saturated inky green color that echoed the iconic privet hedges outside, understanding how dark walls would visually expand the space and give the artwork a fresh perspective. We grounded the room in a thick braided jute that juxtaposed

OPPOSITE: A Giacometti-inspired center table, oversize verdigris mirror, and a mobile-like light fixture balance the volume of the double-height entry while hinting at the eclectic mix of old and new in the rooms that follow. FOLLOWING SPREAD: The furniture placement in the living room encourages easy flow for entertaining. The neutral palette directs all eyes first to the artwork by Jim Welling over the mantel.

PRECEDING SPREAD: The dining room's glossy, hand-glazed walls, custom lacquered dining table, leather-upholstered dining chairs, jute area rug, and contemporary chandelier recalibrate the balance of rustic and refined. ABOVE: Walls drenched in a deep green provide a vibrant backdrop for the artwork by David Hockney. OPPOSITE: The small, custom marble table doubles for intimate meals and larger buffets.

When rooms open organically from one to another and to the exterior, it is important to choose elements of decoration that create visual consistency for comfort but also impart enough contrast to establish differentiation and keep the views interesting.

beautifully against the dark polished dining table that sits beneath a stunning, handcrafted contemporary chandelier.

The family room connects the kitchen, living room, and a screened porch that, furnished for living and dining plein air, became central to their lifestyle. We positioned the family room's sectional sofa to reinforce these spatial relationships and help define the open, connected spaces.

The primary suite upstairs came with significant architectural issues that needed to be addressed. We stripped this room down to its studs and reconceived the space, adding ribbonlike wooden strap work and a subtle handglazed wall finish that appear to wrap the space up like a gift and create a sense of softness and intimacy.

This house now welcomes guests with open arms and major artwork. When the couple is home alone, the open plan allows them to be in separate rooms yet remain connected.

OPPOSITE: The island serves as the kitchen's hub and includes handy storage for favorite cookbooks, among other things. The triple light from Ann Morris amply illuminates the work surface below. Family and friends can easily pull up to the counter to provide conversation and company during meal preparation.

RIGHT: The family room, which connects the living room to the kitchen and screened porch beyond, offers an extension of the living room's palette. The blend of contemporary and vintage continues with a custom L-shaped sectional dressed in a comfy wool and cotton chenille; its placement keeps sight lines open to the kitchen as well as directed toward the TV on the opposite wall. The rounded corners of the vintage honed-travertine coffee table fit with the sofa's relaxed interior angle. Unlined linen panels hanging from custom blackened bronze hardware softly filter the glow of summer sun.

OPPOSITE: We added ribbonlike strap work and a hand-painted crosshatch glaze to create a warm, enveloping architecture in the completely reconfigured primary bedroom. Plush fabrics—including silk mohair velvet, natural linen, and wool—sit below a sculptural chandelier by Aspara. ABOVE: The oak bed frame with nickel and bronze campaign-style hardware we designed for our Century Furniture collection grounds the room.

ABOVE: The material mix continues in the screened porch off the family room. With teak furnishings for plein air living and dining, this has naturally become one of the clients' favorite spaces for entertaining—and relaxing, too. OPPOSITE: The nest-like lantern is an all-weather wonder that beautifully blends with the cedar shingle siding.

COUNTRY CHARM

Being part of a team that brings a client's vision into reality over the course of decades is a dream. That's been our fortunate experience working with Anna Wintour on her country compound on Long Island's East End. From the start, she envisioned the interiors of the nineteenth-century cottages and farm outbuildings we helped transform into guest quarters to be rustic and hand hewn in the best ways, and full of vibrant color, pattern, and texture. Dedicated to her vision, Anna assembled a core group to help realize and maintain the dream, including a master craftsman, a decorative painter, a garden designer, an architect, and us. Together with Anna and the team we continue to focus on these properties today.

The first tiny cottage here—lovingly called Roosevelt Cottage because Eleanor allegedly spent time here—encompassed an intact portion from the 1830s and an ungainly addition from the 1980s. We endeavored to restore it to the original cottage foundation and brought the interior up to date, keeping as much as possible of its original pine board walls, beadboard ceilings, and rustic beams. We drenched the library in red and gray and opted for a pale green wash in the living room. The kitchen is more today than yesteryear, with new planks in between the original beams, and new shelves and cabinets decoratively distressed to look as if they've been there forever. Mint green frescoed walls frame the breakfast room. The raw plank table with its brilliant fuchsia runner sits on a high-gloss floor. The balance shifts in the dining room, with terra-cotta frescoed walls, a bold floral tablecloth, and an antique light fixture. The primary bedroom shows the inherent charm of a collected interior. Though the mix may appear completely spontaneous, we deliberately calculated its laid-back look.

The Moss Barn, originally an agricultural building, adjacent to the cottage, required complete reimagination and renovation. We created interior texture and patina with applied knotty pine boards and trim. The balance of the elements—contemporary floral patterns, traditional stripes, painted Swedish antiques, a salvaged soapstone industrial sink, hand-glazed checkerboard tiles—bring the romance and charm of Anna's vision of a bucolic country estate to life.

OPPOSITE: With its antique Swedish chair, red-painted planking, contrasting gray cabinetry, and patterned linen roman shade, the library offers a snapshot of this cottage's casual chic, expressive charm, and sophisticated but relaxed country aesthetic.

RIGHT: The living room shows the patina of age in its pine plank walls, intimate dimensions, original floorboards, and ceiling beams. The furnishings incorporate pieces from today and yesterday, including an ottoman and armchair from George Smith, a pair of vintage wicker armchairs, and a contemporary sofa. The colors and patterns, the floral curtains, the striped pillows, and the kilim-covered ottoman look spontaneous but are highly considered.

A Place in the Country
CLASSIC COUNTRY
NUREYEV
SPENCER TRACY
A LIFE OF PICASSO
JOHN RICHARDSON
AMERICAN STYLE
ALT 365
ANDRÉ LEON TALLEY
DREAMS
CAROLINA HERRERA
OSCAR NIGHT - VANITY FAIR
CHRISTOPHER PLUMMER
WALT DISNEY
STRAVINSKY
LA BELLE FRANCE
A REPORTER'S LIFE

OPPOSITE AND ABOVE: Mirroring the original spaces' quality and era helps highlight the cottage's inherent charm. FOLLOWING SPREAD: Rusticated, intentionally distressed kitchen cabinets reflect existing hand-hewn elements throughout. PAGES 244–45: Hand-applied finishes create texture in the new rooms. The antique hutch belonged to Bunny Mellon. PAGES 246–47: In classic country style, rattan, ticking, and florals converge in the primary bedroom.

RIGHT: The low door was the entry to the original farm outbuilding; the tall side door was added in its conversion to guest quarters. We applied knotty pine boards to the walls and ceiling to create texture and character where none previously existed. PAGES 250 AND 251: Painted Swedish antiques add romance—and color, of course—to this interior's air of casual sophistication. Contemporary floral prints from Radish Moon dress the windows and bed pillows, while hand-painted lampshades add whimsy.